YET

THE PROMISE IN HABAKKUK FOR THOSE IN TRANSITION

About This Devotional

Yet is for you if you're walking through a season of transition—graduating from school or starting a new job, living alone for the first time or moving in with a spouse, beginning a new relationship or mourning a break-up, becoming a parent, moving to a new city, or feeling like everything is changing around you. The ever-changing circumstances of life can leave you grasping for solid ground when the world shifts beneath your feet. Times of transition—living in the in-betweens of life—can shake you to your core.

In this devotional, you will learn how the prophet Habakkuk begins by taking his complaints and honest heart to God and ends in rejoicing—not because of his circumstance, but because of the character and love of God. Each week will walk through part of the book of Habakkuk along with supplemental Scriptures and guided questions for reflection and prompting you to practice thankfulness. Yet encourages you to experience your daily life with Jesus while giving you a safe space to celebrate and grieve all of life's changes. You'll find that the same God you know—or have heard of—is faithful, true, and good in this season of transition, that his heart and love for you is consistent in every season, and that the love of Christ for you will fuel you daily and free you forever.

YET

THE PROMISE IN HABAKKUK FOR THOSE IN TRANSITION

Erica Boden

HR

Yet; The Promise in Habakkuk For Those in Transition

Published by Hosanna Revival in Cincinnati, OH

Cover design: Hosanna Revival

First printing 2021
Second printing 2022
Third printing 2023

All emphasis in Scripture quotations have been added by the author.

Printed in China

To Sophia. I love the way you love Jesus.

TABLE OF CONTENTS

TABLE OF CONTENTS

A Note from the Author

Hey. I'm so grateful you've picked up this book.

I'm going to ask you to be honest throughout these pages. We are going to look at Scripture, the most accurate account of human history and the story of God. It's a safe space, held between you and Jesus, here and heaven. When you write down how you feel or what you have experienced, there are no right answers.

Since I'm going to ask you to reflect and share about your life, here's the low-down on me.

At 22 years old, like many people, I graduated from college. A few months later, unlike many people, I moved to Bulgaria. While my life changed drastically as I learned new languages and discovered an absence of toilet seats, my friends' lives were also changing simultaneously.

All at once, it seemed, marriage bells rang. We were starting jobs. We were painting, dreaming, trying to pay bills. We were applying to grad programs, getting rejected, and then applying again. We were sitting with cancer-ridden loved ones. We were seeing positive signs on pregnancy tests and wondering how different a baby shower would be from a bachelorette party.

There were moments—so many moments—of great joy. There were also moments of great pain. Of wondering how life changed so much, of moving to a third apartment, of craving something consistent among the ever-changing politics, partners, places, and plans.

During a weekend trip with a few college friends, we looked around at each other and asked, *Why didn't anyone tell us it would be this hard?*

Yes, people told us things would change and life would look different, but no one mentioned the possible identity crisis, conflicting emotions, and the chasm between our starry-eyed dreams and reality.

Then, I remembered: we've already been walking through transitions like this. You don't have to move to Bulgaria to experience the growing pains of adjustment. It was like moving to college and eating dinner alone for the umpteenth night in a row. It came with friends in high school adjusting to having divorced parents, sports seasons ending in college, and significant others changing—or cementing.

It is neither wholly good nor bad, neither black nor white. This is life in the gray area.

As humans, our souls crave being known and loved; we are made that way. All the while, life sets us up for a roller coaster of change. We are typically preparing for a transition, in a transition, or adjusting to our post-transition "new world." None of us are exempt from a life of continual change, and none of us walk through transitions without receiving a scratch or bruise—not even the most resilient, adventurous, laissez-faire of us.

I have spent much of my life in gray areas of transition, even when life appears stable from the outside. I think many people feel the same. We live in the "already" and the "not quite yet"—the present today, preparing for tomorrow, and maybe frustrated at the past. We are constantly moving, continually in motion, and it is unlikely that will change anytime soon.

In the midst of swirling change, God is our constant. When the world moves and we are laid off, or when the ground shakes and we lose a dear friend, God remains the same: unchangeable.

You may not know God. Or maybe you know him and you don't like him a whole lot. Or maybe you know him and love him and know God is unchangeable.

This is for all of you.

It is one thing to *know* God never changes, and it is another thing to *experience it*. To live it. To walk in it daily. To know he is steady when everything else swirls about and flips upside down. To know he is peace when anxiety creeps up. To know he is present when isolation rains down on us.

Have you ever been told, “God is good, just trust him”? Have you ever thought, Yes, I *know* that, but I cannot *feel* that? Those nonchalant Christan sayings—while they may sometimes be true—can be insulting or frustrating when life seems to be caving in.

This is for you, too.

Whether I was in high school, college, or the continuum of adulthood, I wanted a manual of sorts. A quick guide to pulse check if I’m doing this okay, if God is still with me, and vice versa. I think many people feel this way.

This devotional is far from a *how-to* guide. It’s not a manual. I’m kind of directionally challenged (unless I’m driving), and all I really know is the best thing you can offer people when life seems gray is something constant: Jesus.

This is my best offering of him to you. This is a resource that is going to walk consistently with you through inconsistent times. It’s a way for young and old alike to know they have an anchor, a hope, a constant, a steady in a malleable situation. I’m praying for you.

In him,

Erica

Why Habakkuk?

I stumbled upon Habakkuk when it was about -14° Celsius (≈7° Fahrenheit), and the people I interacted with were mainly 13-19 years old who called me Miss, Teacher or Учителка (Bulgarian for teacher, pronounced in my mind: ew-chee-tell-ka). I was looking for a book of the Bible, something I could read through quickly, and Habakkuk jumped out as it was fairly short. The winter was dragging on as my desire to spend time in Scripture was fizzling out. Exhausted from my attempts at sleeping (the nightly four layers and creaky space heater weren't a winning combination), I debated not reading it. The Old Testament sometimes scares me, if I'm being honest, and I wasn't looking to feel more intimidated than I already did on a daily basis.

When I was about to flip past it, I read one of the first headings: *Habakkuk's Complaint*.

I didn't know the Bible had any variation of the word *complain* in it, so I was interested. It was the first reminder in a long time that I recalled relating to people in the Bible. The book, while short, had layers unraveling the *realness* of the Father to me again. My Father was approachable and wanted to be approached by me, even if I was feeling off.

Here's some quick background information to help explain some context for what you're going to be reading over the next several weeks:

Habakkuk is one of the twelve minor prophets in the Old Testament (alongside Hosea, Joel, Amos, etc.). In the Hebrew Bible, these twelve minor prophets are considered one big book, called "The Twelve."[1] We do not have a lot of information about who Habakkuk was, but he's introduced as a prophet, so we know he was someone who taught the will of God.

Habakkuk was active around 600 BC, which is 600 years before Jesus was born. Given that, Jesus returning or "the end" of the suffering wasn't exactly in sight yet. There wasn't a grandiose light at the end of the tunnel, and as Habakkuk looked around at the state of the world, it was evil and dark.

In 722 BC, God used Assyria to punish Israel by destroying the northern kingdom. God's people remained faithful. During the time Habakkuk prophesied, the Babylonian army tore through the land God gave his people, leaving disastrous damage. God was now using Babylon (Chaldea) to punish Assyria and Judah.[2]

Habakkuk felt like God was silent and not present while people and nations—specifically the Babylonians/Chaldeans—continued

1 *For more information, see Shawn Aster, "The 12 Minor Prophets," My Jewish Learning. Last accessed January 27, 2022, https://www.myjewishlearning.com/article/the-12-minor-prophets/.*

2 *Most of the background information for Habakkuk came primarily from Chuck Swindoll, "Habakkuk," Insights on the Bible. Last accessed January 27, 2022, https://www.insight.org/resources/bible/the-minor-prophets/habakkuk.*

to get away with destruction. (Babylonians and Chaldeans are used interchangeably throughout the book, referring to the evil people of Babylon.)

Habakkuk, a faithful, God-following person, wondered what God's plan was. When Habakkuk looked around, he saw God's people suffering. He wanted to know what God was doing, so he asked God. What we see unfold in the book of Habakkuk is exciting, reminding us of hope, faith, and a caring God.

How to Use This Devotional

We will read a full book in the Bible, Habakkuk, with supplemental texts and Scripture along the way. Even if your world feels changed or different, and you're just trying to feed your kids and not lock your keys in your car, you will get to read an entire Old Testament book by the end of this.

I'm not trying to surprise you, so here is a tentative plan for each day of the week, numbered 1 through 7. You can choose when you want to "start" your week. If you know the weekdays are hectic, maybe do some of the study parts on the weekend. If Sundays are your most free day, I recommend kicking it off with day one, as you'll read the entire text for the week on day one.

As a note, I read the English Standard Version of the Bible (ESV). Sometimes I might reference a specific line of Scripture or a few words from it, and if it varies from what you read, just know we have different translations! All translations will work great with this devotional.

How to Use This Devotional | Structure

Day 1 | Assessment: Take inventory of where you are spiritually, think about what's on the docket for the week, and read the entire portion of Habakkuk assigned for the week.

Days 2 - 6 | Study: Read smaller portions of the week's Habakkuk reading, additional Scripture, then answer and pray through the relevant questions.

Day 7 | Reflection: Re-read select verses from the week, reflect, share thankfulness, and praise God.

INTRODUCTION

Introduction

When I think of end caps on the chapters of my life, they are vivid.

I see the shiny, crinkly confetti falling at high school graduation. I feel the gray, wiry carpet I fell on when I got a call that my friend died. I taste my face's salt as I hobbled across the finish line of a marathon. The awkward first night after my parents dropped me off at college alone, with a bowl of Honey Bunches of Oats, thinking, *now what*? The first day of a new job. The first day after a break-up.

Yes, these events are significant for what they are. Some are the culmination of years of academic work or physical training. Some, though, weren't chosen nor prepared for. They were flung upon us, despite not wanting to know what adjusting to life—without a friend, a significant other, or the job that felt promised—looked like.

Moreover, these events are significant for what they represent: the entering of a transition season—a gray area of life, the muddled, maybe even the mess itself. The areas of life that may come with both joy and sadness, and maybe both in the same day. Heck, it could be multiple times a day.

The emotions of life's transitions are seen in the elation of commencement and the heartbreak of leaving beloved college roommates. It's when you get a new boss at work, and it's neither good nor bad, but both: it's bittersweet. It's the reality that being married might be so fun, but living with another person might be so hard. The clarity of feeling called and the confusion when you answer the call. It can be felt in groups of people or in the isolating silence of your 600-square-foot apartment. These areas of life are neither black nor white. It's the gray area.

We spend a lifetime full of preparing, transitioning, and adjusting to a new normal—then getting ready to do it again.

I began following God when I was seventeen. As a believer and lover of Jesus, I knew God walked with me. I knew Scripture was filled with stories of God walking with his people, never leaving nor forsaking them. Yet, it wasn't until years later, when I moved home from Bulgaria after a year of living, teaching, breathing, and being there, that resilience failed, and I realized just knowing wasn't going to suffice. Somewhere between reverse culture shock, trying to merge onto highways, and sheer exhaustion, mere knowledge couldn't keep me from sobbing in a privacy booth at work or snapping at an innocent barista.

When life turned on its head, I needed to know *and* believe God was there. I needed to see him *in* it with me, not looking back in a hindsight-is-20/20 kind of way. If he is the Prince of Peace, the Ultimate Healer, and the Great I AM, then I need to find him in the transition daily. I need to believe he, in fact, would be there—more vividly than the end caps in my life.

The end caps haven't closed a door without the Lord opening another.

In the midst of new zip codes, new last names, new diagnoses, God is *with* you. He sees you. He walks with you. He carries you.

In the midst of change—whether good or bad, whether chosen or unexpected—will you dare to believe with me he's going to be present?

Transition Time: Where Are You?

As we begin, write down what you are walking through. This could be where you're coming from or going to, where you physically are, or how you're hoping to grow. If you don't know where you are or where you're going, that's okay! This is just for you to have as an initial pulse check. After you finish Habakkuk, this pulse check will allow you to reflect on how you've seen God the past several weeks.

What transition or life change are you currently experiencing?

How would you describe your current relationship with God?

WEEK ONE

DAY ONE | Assessment

I thought I was walking fast, but the consumption of six bags of mini pretzels and the lack of sleep made me feel like a groggy fifth-grade girl meandering and shuffling her feet through the crowded airport.

My eyes were blinking faster than my heart was beating as I scanned the approaching open space, looking for two middle-aged people I fondly call Mom and Dad.

My panting eyes met my mom's.

I was home.

....

"Take the next exit . . . now, Mom! Turn right!"

I joyously sat in the backseat, laughing as my mom flung our white Ford Flex off the interstate heading toward the building with red cursive font. Bags slid across the floor of the trunk. I looked down at my watch. It was 10:25 a.m., and the minute hand was rounding for home. I had five minutes until breakfast ended, and I had spent the last year dreaming of this moment.

We were going to make it.

Eight minutes later, we had finally made it to the front of the Chick-fil-A line, and a woman was telling me that it was past breakfast hours, something about hash browns not being available, and she was very, very sorry. Other than that, I don't really know what happened because I began, well, crying.

I'm an adult woman, back on American ground permanently, crying in a fast food restaurant.

I walked out of the line as my mom began explaining to the cashier her daughter just got off an airplane from Bulgaria, and she was hopeful they could *make one more batch of hash browns, thank you very much.*

"I'll order some, too!" a man from the back of the line bellowed, as my mom made our case.

Four chicken minis, a couple boxes of hash browns, and a huge iced coffee later, we were back in the safety of the Flex.

As happy and content as the crispy, golden brown, hashbrowny outside made me feel, causing a salty smile I hadn't had for quite some time, I couldn't help but feel immense shame and embarrassment for breaking down within my first hour home. *Get a grip*, I thought to myself.

Like many people, I don't feel immediate peace when I begin a new chapter. There's whiplash in my emotions and speed bumps in my heart. I just cycled through a ton of emotions I experienced above: excitement, sadness, and embarrassment are a few.

Pulse Check: ***How do you currently feel about life?*** *Jot down a few words or phrases below.*

Looking at your life, or the past few weeks, how do you feel when your life is in transition?

How do you view God when your life is in transition?

This week we will study verses 1:1-11 in the book of Habakkuk. Go ahead and read these verses now, and describe what stands out to you.

DAY TWO | Study

Read Habakkuk 1:1-4

What does Habakkuk feel in verse 2?

Write down a time where you felt like Habakkuk in verse 2.

When have you communicated (or felt like communicating) with God as Habakkuk does here?

How do you usually communicate with God?

The season you are currently in may bring a lot of emotions to the surface, some that could be entirely new. One of the most complex things about moving home from Bulgaria was knowing I felt called back to America, but not feeling remotely comfortable back home. It began a season of contrast: joy and frustration. God made us with the ability to feel so many emotions, and he wants to hear about them. God wants to hear how you are really doing, not a buttoned-up, perfectly poised version of how you're feeling.

Read Isaiah 62:6-7.

In Isaiah 62:6-7, it says to give the Lord no rest with your words. He loves the sound of your voice. He loves hearing you pray or talk to him; he waits to hear from you or answer your questions.

We can call it complaining; or, with some days and in some situations, we can just call it being transparent. This honesty is not reckless, though. Like a healthy relationship or a friend you love, we do not get to talk without listening. We certainly don't hastily shout and walk away (even though God can handle our outbursts). We can speak to God honestly, while still respecting who he is.

If you were communicating honestly with God, what is something you'd tell him?

Read 1 John 4:16.

According to 1 John, ***what is God?***

Consider your life at the moment. What is another word that represents who God is to you?

DAY THREE | Study

Read Habakkuk 1:1-4

Habakkuk was living and preaching during uncertain times, and he had questions for God, like *why?* And, later, *how long?* These questions show the urgency of Habakkuk's questions, the intensity of his pain.[1] Habakkuk's questions may stem from a place I have visited often, perhaps a place you are right now: the island of feeling forgotten by God.

My journey back into America felt like falling off of a tightrope, hitting a trampoline, and trying to land my flailing body gracefully, upright and feet-down onto the skinny rope. All the while, I watched my friends appear to transition seamlessly. I wondered if God had forgotten me. I doubted his love for me. I questioned if I were really supposed to be here.

In verse 3, Habakkuk asks the Lord specifically why he sees inequity (injustice). He feels justice is gone, and he thinks God is not listening to his pleas for help.

How do you feel God's presence (anything goes: song, nature, friends, prayer, or another way the Father reveals himself)?

1 *This opening statement is cited from Pastor Tyler St. Clair's sermon titled "Why and How Long?" Last accessed January 27, 2022, http://cornerchurch313.org/media/398371-1580095-2645299/why-and-how-long.*

Like Habakkuk's questions for the Lord, what is a question you have for God right now?

What is something challenging about your current transition and journey?

Habakkuk prays for God to show up, for God to be seen! Habakkuk asks if God is still good in a world that has so much evil and is entrenched and covered in sin. He's honest, begging God to move. As we soon see, the Lord will answer Habakkuk.

Read Revelation 3:20.

As we've written out above, we have questions for God. That's okay. We also know God is love. It's okay to still have questions for a God whom you know loves you. As humans, we have the ability to experience confidence and questioning: again, those conflicting emotions. We have the ability to not feel good, and yet know God is still good.

Although transitions can be incredibly challenging, they often come bearing the promise of exciting things to come. Maybe for you it isn't excitement, but a feeling of deep peace. Rather, this transition could bring a new way to experience the Father, or bring a new routine into your schedule.

What is something good about your current transition and journey?

If you are struggling to see God today, I invite you to pray this with me. However you feel comfortable praying, whether it's writing it below, saying it out loud, or whispering it in your mind:

God, I ask to see you today. I understand I may not have all the answers or feel completely steady, but I ask to see your love for me today. Thank you for welcoming my questions, my voice, my very self. I trust you are working in me. Amen.

DAY FOUR | Study

Read Habakkuk 1:1-4

Rewrite Habakkuk 1:2-3 in your own words.

Read Psalm 34:8.

According to Psalm 34, ***what is God?***

Read Psalm 46:1.

According to Psalm 46, ***who is God?***

Consider your life at the moment. What is another word that represents who God is to you?

As noted yesterday, we have the ability to not feel good, and yet know that God is *still* good. We also wrote down questions we have for God. Asking God questions and allowing ourselves to tell the Lord our emotions may be a new experience.

Fortunately, though, God does not experience the uncertainty we do. We can feel unsure about a situation or season, but the Lord is never unsure. We might not understand the world or our surroundings, but the Lord understands everything. We may not see the other side yet, but the Lord sees it all. Our confidence comes from God, trusting these things are true about God, not our own understanding.

Read Philippians 1:6.

Paul, in Philippians, tells us something of which he is sure: God, who has begun a good work in you, will bring it to completion through Jesus Christ. God is currently working in you and will continue working in you until we are in heaven with him. Paul is sure of this, which allows him to live with confidence in God.

Reflect on where you are today. What is something you are sure of or confident in during this transition?

What is something you are sure of and confident in about God?

We have voiced and identified our different feelings, as well as different characteristics God has, like being loving and good. Those things may not always look the same, but we have a loving Father who wants to speak peace and safety into anger and fear. We have a God who is trustworthy and good, even when the world doesn't feel good.

DAY FIVE | Study

Read Habakkuk 1:1-11

This week began by reading Habakkuk 1:1-11. Let's quickly zoom out. *What are the two headings you see in this Scripture?*

1.

2.

I love seeing these two things together: Habakkuk complains, then the Lord answers. Habakkuk, crying out to God in honest frustration, gets a response from him. While it looks immediate here, we do not know the exact time or duration that passed between Habakkuk calling on the Lord and receiving an answer from God. Yet, this gives me great hope. At a zoomed-out view, we see the Most High King answer one of his children's complaints. That's pretty powerful.

Read Habakkuk 1:5-11.

Growing up, I was always told you get out what you put in. (Does anyone else hear their high school sports coaches yelling that? Just me?) Only honesty can truly invite people near your heart. While God is always honest, even if we aren't, being honest with him invites him near our hearts, making our human selves more susceptible to looking for him around us. After Habakkuk asks God why and how long, God answers. Even if we do not audibly hear God's response in a present moment, he will answer.

Prayer turns into answers; speaking with God is action.

Write down verse 5.

Look among the nations, and see;

Turn back to page 25 of day one this week, what did I say to myself in the last line?

While this is an old, yet commonly-spoken phrase among siblings, this is also a clear picture of my self-reliance. I walked into a new environment, and instead of asking God to reveal himself to me, I reminded myself *I have this*. Once I get a grip, I will be okay because I am strong. This contradicts verse 5, where God tells us he is doing the work.

Read 2 Corinthians 12:9-10.

Recount something that has challenged, frustrated, or stretched you during your transition.

Explain how you reacted in the above scenario. Do you see yourself trying to "fix" or handle these challenges, or asking the Lord to help?

While verse 5 is one of the most commonly and happily-quoted verses—speaking of God's greatness and magnitude of what he will do for us—verses 6-11 are a bit less cheery. God's response to injustice, at this time, is letting them know there's more coming: more wrong is coming to their world.

While we don't know what will happen tomorrow, God does not promise a painless life. *In this season where the ground may be shifty at times, what would it look like to be content?*

DAY SIX | Study

Read Habakkuk 1:5-11

We are going to read a passage from the book of Job. Like Habakkuk in verses 1-4, Job is also honest and real with God. Before our next reading, let's begin with some quick background information.

The book of Job was written between the years of 1500 and 500 B.C. This book looks into God allowing a good, God-following man—Job—to suffer. It tells the story of a man who believed God was good and clung to that truth as his world turned upside down and his friends left him. Through Job's commitment to God, Job's deep faithfulness to the Father is revealed.[2]

Satan has just taken Job's property—his oxen, his home—and his children. Let's read Job's response.

Read Job 1:20-22.

Write down verse 22.

In all of this—losing his family, friends, home, oxen—Job doesn't charge God with wrongdoing. Job doesn't stop following God because he's experiencing loss on earth. Here we see an intensely

2 This background information for Job is found in the book introduction for Job in my Hosanna Revival ESV Journaling Bible®, published by Crossway.

suffering man be honest with God without spitefully accusing him of messing up. If we're being honest with ourselves, we have all probably been in situations where we've let our anger get the best of us. Have you ever hit one too many red lights when you're already running late? If so, you probably know exactly what I mean.

I do *not* excel at *not* sinning.

When have you lost something or someone you love? Maybe you're experiencing this right now, or maybe you've experienced it in the past. How did you react to that? How did you commune and communicate with God during that?

As we talked about on the first day, we have a lot of feelings. The world can be complex, and the world can be emotion-driven. God and his word are constant.

Read Psalm 116:5.

What does Psalm 116:5 say ***that God is?***

What is another word God is to you right now?

You don't have to write anything down now, but what would it begin to look like to bring God deeper into this season of transition? What would it look like to look to God? To converse with him more, to lean on him?

Pray and contemplate on this today. Consider asking the Spirit to reveal to you where you try to carry yourself or where you've charged God incorrectly with wrongdoing.

DAY SEVEN | Reflection

I have not wept in a Chick-fil-A since that hot July day. My mom hasn't had to jump to my defense. I don't feel embarrassed for thinking my world might crumble without breakfast.

As wild as it felt in the moment, looking back, I think I was doing the best with what I had at that time. Was my best glamorous? Nope. Did my best involve being eloquent? Nope. Was my best as kind or as loving as I want to be? Nope.

But fresh off an international plane and with my emotions jumbled, like the clothes in my suitcase, my best was what it was.

The days and year following my incident at Chick-fil-A were not absent of pain. I didn't meet a local or fall in love or suddenly prance back onto the tightrope without pit stains. When all was said and done, though, a few short years later, there was more joy than pain in my transition back to American life.

A week is not equivalent to years, and it may feel like you are in the middle of your story—squashed between two chapters and unsure of which way is up.

What would it look like to pause when you feel anxiousness, frustration, or apathy creep in and remind yourself of who God is? Reflect on what we have read this week, and write down the characteristics of who God is.

Read Habakkuk 1:5.

After reading this verse again, what stands out to you? What does this verse reveal about the character of God?

Read Psalm 34:4-7.

Thanksgiving + Prayer

Here we see the Lord answering those who seek them, delivering them from their fears. He hears his children and saves them from their troubles. *What is a prayer for this week? Before you ask your requests of God, honor and glorify who he is in thanksgiving. Use the below phrases as prompts for your thanksgiving and prayer.*

Jesus, I am thankful for...

Father, I ask...

Write down a word or phrase for your upcoming week. Not what you feel in this moment, but a word or two to remember who God is. Example: Peace.

For this light momentary affliction is preparing for us an eternal weight of glory beyond all comparison, as we look not to the things that are seen but to the things that are unseen. For the things that are seen are transient, but the things that are unseen are eternal

- 2 Corinthians 4:17-18

WEEK TWO

DAY ONE | Assessment

I exhaled hard and long, feeling the rush of hot air tickle my upper lip as it flowed out of my nose. I finished my work day right as the clock sauntered past five, and releasing pent-up air in such a loud manner signified to me, and my rumbling laptop, that we were done for the day. Rest awaits.

It was early fall, which meant we still had light outside at six o'clock and even seven o'clock in the evening. Working at a computer most of the day had somehow turned me into a part-time weather and season aficionado, as those were the two variables determining my post-work activities. The weather was getting chilly, which meant it was the perfect time to tie back my hair and head out onto the pavement.

I started running when I was in seventh grade. I was a *slightly*-above-average runner, and I really enjoyed running because hand-eye coordination was not required. It quickly became a social outlet, as my friends and I would run slowly to chat, catching up on our classes and friends, and ignoring the stacks of homework awaiting us.

While I still train for races today, running has become more of a methodical stress outlet. It's my time away from screens, turning away from the blue light to face the natural light.

I headed out for my usual route. Eighty seconds into my run, not even halfway into Eric Church's "Springsteen" blaring through my headphones, my toe nicked broken concrete on the old sidewalk.

Suddenly, I flew through the air—my body became parallel to the ground for a split-second before crashing onto the concrete. Realizing the impending crash, I threw my phone attempting to free both of my hands to break my fall. My body splatted onto the rocky surface: inflicting raspberries, ripping skin, and causing blood to roll down my shins. The falls little kids can walk off aren't as simple for an adult to rise from.

As the skin on my hands hung off my palms, my pride evaporated, and I laid face-down on the concrete. After a moment of wiggling my fingers, I rolled over. I was lying on my back, gathering enough composure to stand. I stood up, ever so slowly. Looking down, I took inventory of my busted-open kneecaps as I heard a neighbor approach me.

"You okay?" she asked.

My neighbor helped me sit on her porch while she fetched water and bandaids. She dabbed my legs with hydrogen peroxide, letting my eyes shut while my scraped body—and pride—began to recover.

Running is not new for me, as I've moved in that pendulum motion for well over a decade now. For something so routine and simple in my life, I still fell and face-planted on a normal day. Sure, maybe I could've picked up my feet more or not run with my phone in my hand, but sometimes even things that are second nature to us can cause challenges.

When have you felt like you face-planted, whether that be literal or metaphorical?

How do you view God after you splat or struggle?

Read Habakkuk 1:12-2:5.

As we prepare to study this section of Habakkuk for the remainder of the week, what initially stands out to you from these verses?

DAY TWO | Study

Habakkuk 1:12-2:5, which you read yesterday, shows Habakkuk's second complaint and the Lord's second answer. In my ESV Bible, the Lord's second answer is headlined: "The Righteous Shall Live by His Faith."

Before we jump into the study today, what does it mean to you to "live by faith"?

These verses in Habakkuk 1 and 2 show God and Habakkuk in a back-and-forth conversation. It reminds me of conversations I had with my parents growing up.

I'd ask, "Mom, can I come home at midnight tonight?"

She'd smile softly, "No, sweetie. That's too late. Why do you need to be out until midnight on a Thursday, Erica?"

I'd plead, "That's when everyone else is allowed to stay out. What about 11:45 p.m.?"

Now, she chuckles under her breath, "10:00 p.m., Erica. I don't care what everyone else is allowed to do. You have homework and it's a school night."

Even if it wasn't the answer I wanted, my mom engaged in the conversation, wanting the best for me and caring for me well. However, the conversation between God and Habakkuk is much more important and symbolizes more than a highschooler wanting to stay out late. After listening to and receiving God's first answer in Habakkuk 1:5-11, Habakkuk responds to God with more questions. This is significant for many reasons, but two jump out to me:

1. Habakkuk doesn't walk away from God when he doesn't get the answer he wanted.

If you recall, God's answer to Habakkuk wasn't some cookie-cutter cute response (1:6-11). It was the hard reality of, "Hey, I'm here, but this may get worse." Instead of walking away or being apathetic, Habakkuk remains faithful (living by faith) and shows up again to ask God more questions.

2. God doesn't walk away from Habakkuk when he is approached with more questions.

God doesn't tire of us or "zone out." He listens, remains, and is ready to walk through our questions with us, whether it is the same thing we've asked before or addressing a new ache.

Read Isaiah 41:10.

What does God promise to do?

Read Habakkuk 1:12-13.

What is Habakkuk asking the Lord for in these verses?

Reflect on where you are today. For what are you asking the Lord?

DAY THREE | Study

Read Habakkuk 1:14-2:1

We see Habakkuk's frustration in these verses. While he didn't walk away from God and continues asking him questions, his confusion is obvious. In Habakkuk's view (v. 13), God is allowing evil, which leaves Habakkuk with more questions for the Lord. We even see Habakkuk start to assume God may not even know what is going on.

What does verse 14 compare men to?

Like one of "the fish of the sea," I have felt small in life, especially in seasons of transition. There's something about moving between two jobs, two relationship statuses, or two locations that can leave you wondering if anyone really knows you or knows what's going on.

Even if friends or family know what's going on, sometimes it's still easy to feel lost in the shuffle. Like Habakkuk, I have been left wondering if God knows what's going on.

In the midst of these two (or three or four) places in our in-between, there are highs and lows, perks and pits. In verses 12-17, Habakkuk questions God, his voice dripping with exhaustion. Habakkuk calls out to God from what I could call a pit.

What does my neighbor ask me on day one this week (page 57)?

After my fall left me humiliated and bleeding on the sidewalk, a neighbor came rushing from across the street, asking if I was okay. In a moment that initially felt only negative, a good thing still emerged. God had a kind neighbor witness my fall (again, ouch to my pride), who immediately came over ready to help.

Transitions are long roads of perks and pits. Some days, or even weeks, may feel amazing. Others may feel awful. Throughout our lives, the movement of leaving one season of life and entering into another brings both joy and sorrow. The perks might be a new start or a new way to hear Jesus, and the pits may include missing and longing for things of the past; feeling wobbly and wondering if Jesus is there.

List some pits of your transition.

Write down some perks of your transition.

Read Proverbs 3:5-6.

Reflect on your day yesterday. Was it full of pits or perks? Perhaps a mixture of both? Write down a moment where you saw or felt the Lord's presence.

DAY FOUR | Study

Read Habakkuk 1:12-2:1

Over the past couple days, we've read and re-read Habakkuk 1:12-2:1. How many questions does Habakkuk ask in his second complaint?

Look back at Habakkuk's first complaint in Habakkuk 1:2-4. How many questions does he ask the Lord here?

What is the significance of this number?

Many scholars have said one of the most powerful numbers in the Bible is the number three. While this number represents the Trinity—the Father, Son, and Holy Spirit—it also represents divine wholeness and completeness.[1]

1 *Hope Bolinger, "What Does the Number Three Signify in the Bible?" Crosswalk.com. Last accessed March 8, 2021, https://www.crosswalk.com/faith/bible-study/what-does-the-number-3-signify-in-the-bible.html.*

When you pray, do you picture God as the Father, the Son, or the Holy Spirit? Scripture gives us many names for God and many pictures of who he is (God is our Father, our friend, our refuge and strength, and so much more).

Write down Habakkuk 2:1.

Habakkuk waits on God. He will wait for the Lord's answer to his complaint, acting as a watchman looking out for God.

Like watchmen, we all wait on God. Whether it is for an answer to a prayer or a question, freedom from an addiction, salvation for a friend, or his holy return one day, we all find ourselves in seasons of waiting. This transition is no different.

Transitions are not a linear path from start to finish; yet, the Lord is steady, and we have direct access to him through prayer. Like I shared in the Introduction section of this devotional, I believe transitions in life are so frequent that we are all typically preparing for a transition, in a transition, or getting out of a transition. Likewise, the unchanging Lord is the Alpha and the Omega, the beginning and the end. God moves in preparation for us, through us, and behind us when we feel still or stuck.

We can see the Lord's hand and presence moving in the world throughout Scripture, and it really stands out to me in the book of Exodus. In Exodus 14, Moses crosses the Red Sea, and God rescues the Israelites from Egypt.

Read Exodus 14:14 and 14:19.

Have you ever had a complaint as you've waited on the Lord? Write down an example from your life in which you were waiting on the Lord.

What would it look like to wait on the Lord in this season of transition?

DAY FIVE | Study

Read Habakkuk 2:2-5

Habakkuk waited, and God answered. Habakkuk still doesn't get the exact answer he was looking for. He asked God why injustice was occurring and why evil people were being lifted high. God does not tell Habakkuk all the answers immediately.

If the vision seems slow, ***what are we supposed to do (2:3)?***

Read Psalm 27:14.

Habakkuk waited for this answer from the Lord. God told him he must wait more, but answers will come. I live in a Western country in the 21st century. My week is seven days and my days are 24 hours. Months are typically 30 or 31 days, and drive-thrus should always take less than ten minutes. I check my phone an obscene amount each day, confirming the time or waiting for someone to text me back. I wear a watch to remind myself of the time and to ensure I can get to where I'm going promptly.

However, God doesn't live by my timeline. In fact, God exists outside of time and space and isn't bound by any world calendar. He most certainly doesn't participate in pushing the clock an hour ahead or behind for Daylight Saving Time. God operates on his timeline.

Waiting has left a bad taste in my mouth for years. I picture the line at a Disney World roller coaster on a Saturday at noon: endlessly long and out of my control. I simply stand there, refreshing the same apps on my phone, twiddling my thumbs away. This, again, is my 21st century worldly waiting.

We get to *actively* wait on God. I say actively because waiting isn't merely sitting on our hands; it's allowing space for God to move and guide us. Waiting can feel frustrating at times, yet we have the ability to have gratitude. We can know where we are in this moment, long for things of the past, and still wait on God.

Do you think God understands what you are going through? Do you believe the Lord has seen you and knows your situation? Why or why not?

Read James 5:7-8.

Share something you could do to honor God and seek peace while you wait.

DAY SIX | Study

Read Habakkuk 2:2-5

In verse 4, God lets Habakkuk know the Chaldeans—the wicked Babylonians—will not escape God's judgment for their sins. Babylon was attempting to establish their own kingdom. They were a prideful group, seeking wealth and riches through dishonest and shady ways.

Write down the last line of verse 4.

God tells Habakkuk not to worry about the Chaldeans and their pride ("puffed up" souls, v. 4); Habakkuk's job is to live by faith. The righteous will live by faith. As Christians and Jesus-loving people, we live by faith. Living by faith means fear, circumstance, sudden desires, and situational moments are not what guide us. Despite what the world around you may look like or say, we trust God in the long-term.

Read Hebrews 11:1-3.

How does Hebrews define faith?

What does this mean for people of faith (v. 2)?

What has faith meant in your life? If that question feels overwhelming, please just explain what faith means for you today.

On day two this week, I asked what it meant for you to live by faith. Godly faith is synonymous with trust. Trusting God—trusting his promise to one day restore our souls—is living by faith. Trust is a Christian buzzword that looks super cute stitched on pillows, but can be really challenging to live out. There's a big difference between talking at God and talking to God, trusting him with your heart. Talking to God is relational: a Father and his child.

Write down something you really want or something that disappointed you during this transition.

What would it look like for you to trust God with that want or disappointment?

Read 2 Corinthians 5:6-7.

Living by faith allows God to guide you. A belief and a knowledge that our lives are purposeful paths to heaven guides us through our time on earth.

Pray for God to grow your trust in him today. Consider asking the Spirit to reveal to you where mistrust with people and things in the world have translated to mistrust with him, your perfect and loving Father.

DAY SEVEN | Reflection

Read Hebrews 11:32-40

Hebrews 11:39-40 always stops me in my tracks. We read about these Old Testament people exhibiting rockstar faith, which allowed them to accomplish great things for God. Heck, through faith people conquered kingdoms and obtained promises. Yet, verses 39 and 40 remind us of this: the faithful ones still suffered hardship. They were persecuted yet remained faithful, believing in God and abiding in God's ways.

Read Habakkuk 2:1.

After reading this verse again, what stands out to you? What does this verse reveal about the character of Habakkuk?

Read Habakkuk 2:4.

After reading this verse again, what stands out to you? What does this verse reveal about the character of God?

Read Romans 8:26-30.

Write down verse 28.

God sent my neighbor for me in the midst of a fall, providing me with a bandage and encouragement. How has God worked something difficult for your good?

Thanksgiving + Prayer

In Romans, Paul reminds us that God works all things together for good for those who love him. *Knowing this, what is something you're praying for this week? Before you ask of God, honor and glorify who he is in thanksgiving. Use the below phrases as prompts for your thanksgiving and prayer.*

Jesus, I am thankful for...

Father, I ask...

Write down a word or phrase for your upcoming week. Not what you feel in this moment, but a word or two to remember who God is.

To be loved but not known is comforting but superficial. To be known and not loved is our greatest fear. But to be fully known and truly loved is, well, a lot like being loved by God. It is what we need more than anything. It liberates us from pretense, humbles us out of our self-righteousness, and fortifies us for any difficulty life can throw at us.

T. Keller

WEEK THREE

DAY ONE | Assessment

It was November, and I had been living in this different yet wonderful country for a couple months now. Most days I had to study my grocery list before feeling confident enough to enter the store. I was nowhere near fully adjusted, but I was trying.

It was autumn in my little town of Silistra, Bulgaria, and while I desperately wanted this place to feel as home-like as I made it seem in my Instagram captions, it didn't quite feel like a place I could meander with full ease. The language barrier was steep and drained me more than I'd like to admit. Parts of the Eastern world are just, well, different than the Western world. The thing I hadn't remotely begun to adjust to were the toilets, also known as squatty potties.

Two months in, I still couldn't figure out how much I needed to squat to pee. You see, when there's a hole in the ground where your sweet, sheltered, American body always had a toilet, you spend a lot of time bending your knees like four inches, and then realizing that didn't work when pee splatters on your ankles. Eventually, you learn to bend your knees all the way to the ground, but you still wonder if you're doing it right.

While I did eventually learn to use them, I didn't love them. My flat was across the street from the high school where I taught my ninth graders. We had 15 minutes between classes, so I realized I could just jaunt home really quickly to pee. And I really had to pee.

The bell rang. I slid my phone in my pocket and walked out of my classroom door. I quickly turned right as I left the room, hurrying towards the stairs, when one of my co-teachers yelled, "Erica," stopping me from my safe getaway. I talked to Ilka for a few moments, shifting my weight from my left foot to my right, then back to my left. I felt my face get flushed, then I interrupted, "Ilka, I was actually on my way out of the building. Mind if we reconvene in a few minutes?"

At this point, I was almost jogging out the door. I took a quick glance left to check for traffic, before shuffle-running through the crosswalk, knowing I couldn't lift my legs any more, but needing to move like Usain Bolt. I felt sweat roll down my sides as I fiddled with my key at the front door, releasing every English and Bulgarian cuss word I knew. When I finally got into the building, I waited an unbearable 30 seconds for my flat's makeshift lift to come down from the seventh floor. Exacerbated by the time it arrived, I forgot to brace for take-off. I got on and punched the yellow-tinted button where a six should be, but the old lift really jolts as it pulls up.

The sudden jerk was just enough to cause my body to give out. And once I started, I physically couldn't stop. I peed myself, urine rushing down my legs. I stopped peeing the moment I reached the sixth floor. I waddled my way inside of my flat and couldn't comprehend what had happened.

It was 10:53 a.m., and I had filled my elevator with urine. It was 3:56 a.m. where most of my friends were, and that left me feeling truly like I was on the other side of the world, pee-covered, with no one to tell. So I did what every adult would do when they pee their pants: text their family group message, clean and change their pants, and take the stairs on the way down.

Standing in my pee pants in my little apartment, I wanted to text one of my friends. In this horrifyingly embarrassing, shame-ridden moment, I simply wanted to ask someone what to do. I desperately wanted someone to give me an A for my effort in getting back or tell me how to navigate peeing yourself while the rest of your world is sleeping. Instead, I felt the loneliness of my life more than ever. In one of my weirdest life moments, I wanted to reach out to my community.

Community, the idea of a group of believers together, is an emphasized component of the Christian faith. I found myself in Eastern Europe fairly alone, no one to ask advice or call on to clean my (literal) mess with me.

Have you ever been without community before? What was that experience like?

Why do you think God created his people (you and I) to be in community?

Read Habakkuk 2:6-20.

What stands out to you in these verses?

DAY TWO | Study

Pulse Check: *How do you feel this week in your current situation?*

Is this the same answer as week one, last week, or different? What has changed?

If you finished reading the verses from Habakkuk yesterday and (a) didn't understand it, or, (b) thought, *whoa*—you're in good company. The first time I read this, I didn't understand it.

In these verses, the Lord pronounces judgment on Babylon. God is harsh and honest as he addresses sin and brokenness. God assures (and reassures) Habakkuk that the evil which immensely frustrates Habakkuk isn't being ignored. One day, God promises, it will stop.

Read Habakkuk 2:6-8.

This is the first of five woes that God speaks over the Chaldeans. These verses highlight their sins. At this point in time, they've conquered nations and taxed them severely. They've taken property and people that are not theirs. They've taken human life. They've gone further than God ever intended them to, attacking Judah and Jerusalem, and that is why this language is intentionally harsh and austere. God tells Habakkuk the Babylonians will not get away with this.[1]

What is something you feel like you have "lost" or had taken from you during your current transition? It can be anything, whether physical, mental, or emotional.

1 *Ken Cayce, "Habakkuk Chapter 2," Discover Books of the Bible. Last accessed January 27, 2022,* https://bible-studys.org/habakkuk-chapter-2/.

Do you believe the Lord watches over and is present in the transitions of your life? If yes, how have you seen that? If no, what would it take for you to believe this?

Read Hebrews 13:14.

Read John 18:36.

What does it mean to you that this world is your temporary home (we have no lasting city; God's kingdom is not of this world)?

DAY THREE | Study

Read Habakkuk 2:9-11

This is the second woe God pronounces, and it focuses on the wealth the Babylonians have dishonestly created for themselves. The Lord says the house they built on theft and pride will eventually come crashing down.

Thus far, we've witnessed Habakkuk wrestle with God yet continuously cling to him. God is now beginning to answer, letting Habakkuk know he sees what's going on there.

How does God seeing Habakkuk apply to you in the midst of chaos and transitions?

What does God's long response tell you about him?

Whether you feel like God sees you in this moment or not, please let me assure you: he does. God sees every breath and every blink. While you may not physically feel like you can sit down and eat dinner with God at this moment, he gives us his people—his body of believers—with whom we enjoy community. Community, which we touched on yesterday, is vitally important to your emotional and spiritual health. Having friends who are truly safe, with whom I can talk and receive loving, biblical advice, has made all the difference in my walk with the Lord.

Read Romans 1:11-12.

Who speaks into your life? Jot down a few names of the people in your close circle, the ones you may go to for a listening ear or for advice.

Have you let them in on your transition? Are they aware of how you feel?

Above, Paul longs to be with people, encouraging faith with one another. If you weren't able to list people above who speak into your life well, have you considered joining a church or small group in your area? If you're not in a place where you could physically join a group of believers (maybe you're in a foreign country), could you try to FaceTime a family member this week?

If you haven't, please pause right now and prayerfully text or call a friend. If you are wading through deep waters and have an available friend, let their steady hand help you find the shore.

Yesterday we ready Hebrews 13:14. Let's read the couple verses after that: **Hebrews 13:15-16.**

These verses directly conflict with what the Chaldeans are doing. They are doing the opposite of good: stealing, not sharing—and pleasing themselves alone. A group of Chaldeans take what is not theirs, directly hurt other people, and prioritize their needs and wants. Every Christmas season, we are bombarded with the message that it is better to give than receive. For eleven months of the year, though, we tend to forget that (people who love Jesus included). Let's live out what Hebrews commends to us here.

Write a praise to God. This could be something with which God has blessed you, something for which you are thankful, or one of the Lord's amazing characteristics for which you are grateful.

Pray about "giving" something away this week. Maybe you're in Bulgaria, and you have nothing to give physically. Maybe you're working 80-hour weeks, and you do not have time to give. Pray about giving away a note, an intentional phone call, or a birthday text to someone you haven't connected with in a while.

DAY FOUR | Study

Read Habakkuk 2:12-14

We've reached God's third woe, saying their forced labor won't last. Verse 12 shows they have built their city and obtained their wealth through bloodshed, which is neither an honest nor righteous way to build a city.

Write down verse 14 here.

The whole world will ***recognize God's glory;*** the Lord will fill the earth. In contrast to the kingdom of Babylon, the Lord's kingdom is everlasting.

How would your life look different right now if the whole world was filled with the knowledge of and a desire for the Lord's kingdom?

Read Hebrews 8:10-12.

Habakkuk and Hebrews both discuss what it means to be with God or against God. In Habakkuk 2:12, we learn people who murder others and build a town with blood are against God. Hebrews 8:10 shares what the Lord declares: "I will be their God, and they shall be my people."

What does it mean to be God's people?

Humans are created for heaven: a perfect and painless and blameless world. This world, that will one day be filled with the knowledge of the Lord's glory, is where we belong. God wants us there with him, and Jesus has paid the price for us to get there. (This truth is found in John 3:16-18.)

The world we live in is neither perfect nor painless. Life is challenging and transitions are hard. Transitions take away your ability to have it all together. I can act like I'm doing great via social media or even over FaceTime, but when I'm standing there in urine-soaked pants needing to be across the street teaching a high school English class, it's hard to make a compelling case for my life being anywhere close to together.

The freedom of Jesus, and of knowing we have a home in heaven, is security far beyond coping during an accident in your elevator. Our security lies in the cross upon which Jesus was crucified. We do not need to "have it all together" or project an image of consistent competence and sufficiency because Jesus is sufficient. He paid the ultimate price. God allowed Jesus to die a gruesome death on the cross so sinful humans would have a chance at heaven, at life evermore with God our Father. Jesus was—and is—our substitute.

What does Jesus' resurrection mean to you today?

What is a façade, like having it all together, that you could prayerfully ask the Lord to take from you during this time, remembering that Jesus is all-sufficient, so we do not have to be?

Read Philippians 3:20.

DAY FIVE | Study

Read Habakkuk 2:15-17

In God's fourth woe, he calls out the Chaldeans for making their neighbors drink until they're drunk, then gawking at their nakedness. I read and reread verse 15, as it painfully reminded me of friends' experiences in college: of peer pressure from "friend" to friend, of men encouraging women to drink, of the poor decisions or impaired judgment that drunkenness can bring, and of injustices brought upon people. The same sin and wickedness covers the earth today as it did thousands of years ago.

Let's look at verse 16. In some versions of the Bible, like the ESV, there's a reference to circumcision. At this time in history, circumcision was a sign of being in covenant with God. Uncircumcision meant they were not God's chosen people nor were they in a relationship with God.

Here, the Chaldeans are seeking glory for themselves, not the Lord. If we love God, our identity is in God, and any glory we may come across in this life should be used to exalt him.

What are key parts of your identity? List all the characteristics, titles, or roles that come to your mind.

How is your current transition affecting your identity?

Read Jeremiah 1:5.

In the above verse, God calls on Jeremiah, a priest and prophet. The verse reveals that God knew us in the womb: that before we were born, he knew us. That's true for all of us, and it means that our identity—our primary value—can only be found in God our Creator.

Our identity is often a compilation of the characteristics we exemplify or the titles we hold. When our identity is rooted in anything other than God, we set ourselves up for failure. Transitions often expose what we value or an area where we have sought our identity.

Read Philippians 1:18-21.

Sin is in the world today not because Jesus isn't present in the world, but because sin resides in our hearts. Jesus, God in the flesh, was beaten, spit on, slandered, and nailed to a cross for us. He was crucified to allow us—sinful, flawed people—to be with him in heaven. He was resurrected and seeks to walk with us daily.

Meditate on the fact that Jesus died once for all, but he's present in our daily lives. What does it look like to honor that and commune with him daily?

Think of this in regards to your current transition. What are you desiring during this in-between season?

Jesus is the ultimate fulfillment of desire. Which of the desires you identified above can be filled through Jesus? Can we search for our desires to be met and satisfied in him?

Read Hebrews 12:28-29.

Zooming out beyond this transition, think about the next five, ten, or twenty years of your life. ***Write down a few desires.***

I have found God often shows us what we really want through our desires. Being honest about the things your heart longs for or finds peace in is crucial, as it allows you to talk with God or community. By vocalizing to God what you long for, you will allow him, or others, to share what you really need or want in Christ.

Pray over the desires you listed above. Ask God to reveal himself as your source of peace in them.

DAY SIX | Study

Read Habakkuk 2:18-20

The last woe God pronounces is idolatry. As we discussed yesterday, many of our desires stem from searching for things only the Lord can provide. We long for things like peace, hope, and steadiness, but those are only truly satisfied in Christ. Idolatry is worshiping, or having extreme love, for something or someone other than God. It is easy to make worldly things our idols, even when we love and look for God. Your phone, your job, even the person you are dating can become an idol. None of those things are bad; in fact, they are all good gifts from God, but when overconsumed or misused, they become idols in our lives. In verse 18, the idol mentioned is a physical piece of wood carved by a man, which people would worship over God.

In my first few months in Bulgaria, I was acutely aware and always thinking about the fact that, *oh, I'm living in* Bulgaria. I couldn't walk to the grocery store unprepared or without having studied the common checkout/cashier questions and my corresponding answers. When I was yelled at during a run, I didn't know if it was a cat call or someone warning me of unsafety. I always felt "on," like at any moment I had to be prepared for a mission. The more I focused and thought about my transition, the bigger Bulgaria became. In turn, the smaller Jesus became. The more I saw and studied my situation, the less I saw and studied God and his word.

In a gradual, yet accidentally-fell-into-it kind of way, transitioning became an idol for me. While my situation was the reality of my day-to-day life, I was not consumed by desiring to see the Lord's goodness in the land of the living. Rather, I was deeply consumed by my desire to be competent, good, and able to live smoothly again. It is not bad to be strategic or proactive, but if it gradually becomes consuming, it is dangerous.

In what part of your situation have you dwelled, perhaps more than you have dwelled in Jesus?

Zoom out and reflect on your days prior to following God. What were the things that consumed your time or your mind?

The Lord isn't threatened by idolatry, but our souls are. God is a jealous God, and is not pleased when we worship anything other than him (Exodus 34:14). Idolatry is also destructive to our relationships; our postures towards things which cannot love us back. In the words of A.W. Tozer, "As God is exalted to the right place in our lives, a thousand problems are solved all at once." [2]

Idols can also validate our independence, causing us to depend more on our abilities than the Lord's generosity and care. Like me acing an interaction at the grocery store or seamlessly buying myself a bus ticket, we far too often see our "own doing" instead of seeing the generosity of the Lord.

Where do you see the generosity of God in your life?

2 *A. W. Tozer, The Pursuit of God (Harrisburg, PA: Christian Publications, Inc., 1948), 104.*

God, our loving Father, adores hearing our voices. As the good, patient, and faithful Father he is, he loves to hear our desires, and he is extravagant in the ways he loves us. That does not mean he always fills our desires as we think they deserve to be filled, but he knows our needs.

Read Isaiah 65:24.

Where we spend our time, thoughts, emotional energy, and exhaustion, is where our treasure is (Matthew 6:21). Let's pray about our transition more than we talk about it or analyze it in our minds.

Pray with reverence and awe today for God to open your eyes to his goodness. Consider repenting (asking God for forgiveness) from the things you've placed above God this week. Ask him to align the desires in your heart to what he desires for you.

DAY SEVEN | Reflection

Read Isaiah 61:1-3

What stands out to you in these verses?

In these verses, Isaiah describes the ministry God has called him to, which would later be fulfilled in Jesus Christ. As people called to reflect the goodness and glory of Christ, how do these verses encourage us to live?

As the plane rumbled gently left-to-right, I heard the pilot murmur something beyond my headphones. We were landing. I had never been to Europe, prior to moving to Bulgaria. The plane buzzed as we prepared to touch down in Warsaw, and, like a sweet child on Christmas, I was filled to the brim with awe and wonder. My first time in a new country, on a new continent. My eyes were glued to the window, wondering what this new world would look like. What would be the first thing I saw upon looking out my window? The first thing my European virgin eyes set their sights on?

A Marriott hotel.

What was different than you expected during your current transition?

Read Habakkuk 2:14 and 2:20.

What is something we can know and expect in God with full certainty?

I experienced so much joy and happiness and deep confusion and sadness in my move. There were so many exciting firsts, and then there were less exciting ones like peeing my pants. The Lord's offer to us is certainty in Christ, peace that transcends understanding, and a hope that is waiting in heaven. Severe culture shock, meanwhile, left me reeling from cultural whiplash.

Read Proverbs 19:21.

How do you feel knowing God's plans for you may be different than what you've conjured up?

Thanksgiving + Prayer

What is a prayer for your week? Before you ask of God, honor and glorify who he is in thanksgiving.

Write down a word or phrase for your upcoming week. Not what you feel in this moment, but a word or two to remember who God is.

Therefore the Lord himself will give you a sign. Behold, the virgin shall conceive and bear a son, and shall call his name Immanuel.

-Isaiah 7:14

WEEK FOUR

DAY ONE | Assessment

My head rested on a pillow as I stretched my legs out, tapping the other end of the love seat. My mind felt numb, but my thumb was moving. Scrolling up and down methodically. It was 1:00 p.m., and I was lying on my burnt orange and brown couch in Bulgaria. Unable to spend my day outside with the subzero temperatures, I spent an exciting day inside, scrolling Instagram.

I usually joke with my friends or sister that there are two types of people in the world: those who stalk themselves on Instagram—scrolling through the depths from high school or college and fondly remembering the glory days—and those who stalk others on Instagram, falling down a hole from advertisements or friends or, well, just random people you follow. This was a rare and luxurious day where I was going to do both.

Feeling a bit narcissistic as I lay there alone, I started with myself. My thumb looked like a well synchronized bouncy ball, nodding up and down as I flew into the depths of my past. I made it back to high school graduation, went through game days from college, a birthday party or two, a summer internship and, gradually, I just froze.

I flew into a headspace I hadn't reached in a while, feeling anxious and unable to identify the root. I wondered if that one girl from high school would recognize me at a Kroger, or if my ex-boyfriend ever thought of me. Not in a weird, miss-me kind of way, but like, did I ever cross his mind? Did my old boss still like me when I didn't come back to work there? Would I ever truly be able to admit that I did care when I learned what's-her-name talked bad about me? I remembered the self-reliance of my past, which now left me drained, unable to be present where I was and fully immersed in the hypothetical opinion of people I didn't communicate with.

I abruptly stood up from the couch and began walking to my closet. Wrapping a scarf around my neck with one hand and holding the back tab on my boot with the other, I bundled up. I shoved my other wool-sock-covered foot down into my boot. Lacing them quickly, I walked outside to the gray sky and frigid air. I began walking around my block, reminding myself it was 6:00 a.m. in America, and it was highly unlikely anyone there woke up thinking about what I did when I was 15 or 19 or 21. I walked faster, trying to separate my body and my mind from a cycle of self-doubt, pushing my feet hard into the snow-covered ground, and feeling my hip flexors tug as I pulled them up.

The more my brain dwelled on the past, the tighter I clutched to square photos that wouldn't serve me. As my thoughts wandered away from my identity in the Lord, insecurities and a desire for approval surfaced.

When your mind wanders, do you dwell more on the past or the future?

Even though no one I knew lived near me, I learned about my deep desire to seek others' approval. I questioned things I couldn't control: was I as kind as I could have been? Did that person ever actually forgive me or did they just accept my apology? It reminded me of several summers back, when I interned at a bank. Determined to succeed, to do well and be polite, I woke up early and stayed up late to ensure every ounce of work got done. I ran on little sleep and stopped running (what I really loved doing), as it was usually dark during the hours I was free. I relied fully on myself, my abilities, and my mind. I knew Jesus loved and cared for me, but he wouldn't be able to fix this spreadsheet for me. During that challenging transition, I learned how independent I like to be—not just from a significant other or family or friends, but, at times, from God.

Has your current transition made you aware of an area of your life that might need healing?

Read Habakkuk 3:1-16.

What stands out to you in these verses?

DAY TWO | Study

Read Habakkuk 3:1-4

In chapter 2 of Habakkuk, God answered Habakkuk's question: he told Habakkuk of the wrath he will bring upon Babylon. In chapter 3, Habakkuk prays to God. Specifically, he now asks God to remember mercy on Israel.

How would you define "mercy"?

Now, look up the definition. How does this affect your reading of Habakkuk?

Have you ever sped while driving? Yes, same. I speed too frequently. Not too far over the limit, but enough for me to feel more efficient or like I'm earning some kind of time back in my day. I pulled into a parking lot recently and, upon putting my car in park, let out a huge gasp as I noticed the police officer across the lot. He was looking at my car, as I had just raced through other parking spots to pull into mine, going over the 15 MPH recommended speed. Undoubtedly, I deserved a warning or a ticket. Mercy.

When was a time someone showed you mercy?

When was a time God showed you mercy?

Write down verse 4 here.

What is the last word of the verse in the ESV?

Verses 3 and 4 show God's power. Verse 3 points to this beautiful fact: God is the Creator, the King, the Owner of all we know and see. God created the heavens and the earth (Genesis 1), which means he is powerful beyond what human minds can conceive.

God is all-knowing, all-loving, and all-powerful. God's right hand can shatter the enemy (Exodus 15:6), which leads me to believe that God is strong enough to hold my life, my broken dreams, and my desired plans.

What does trusting God with your future look like?

Sometimes, to trust God with your future, you have to reflect on your past. Do you trust that Christ has paid for your past? Do you believe every cuss word, speeding ticket, unseen sin, lie, word of gossip, and beyond is forgiven?

Read Ephesians 1:7-10.

DAY THREE | Study

Read Habakkuk 3:5-9

Yesterday we talked about God's power. If you believe God is as powerful as the Bible says he is, then you have no choice but to believe he is fully able to make you new again. You are fully forgiven by God.

Read Isaiah 1:18.

Today, your world may seem crazy. You might be walking through a rocky season of your own or barely holding it together at work. What does the above verse mean to you?

God has the power to wash us clean, to take our sins away and cleanse us. Not only does he have the power to wash sin away, but he loves us so much that he actually desires to wash us clean. He desires to use his loving power for our eternal good, so we can be with him forever.

This section of Habakkuk, and verse 6 in particular, shows us God's power is unmatched. He stands and the earth shakes. God controls all: the hills, the water, the mountains. If God can hold the moon and stars, he can hold you too.

Write an example of a time the Lord has held you or **"cleared a path"** *for you. This can be anything—perhaps he blessed you with great friends or maybe he guided you into a church family that helped grow your faith.*

What does this say about God's power?

What does this say about God's heart?

Read Ephesians 3:14-21.

What does it mean that God is able to do far more abundantly than we could ask or think?

According to Ephesians, we literally cannot grasp how much God loves us. What would you say to God, or how would you respond, knowing that Christ's love surpasses our knowledge?

DAY FOUR | Study

Read Habakkuk 3:10-13

The last line of verse 10 says, "[the deep] lifted its hands on high." The deep refers to the waters of the Red Sea and/or the Jordan River.[1] It implies this deep, huge body of water is lifting its hands high. I picture a crowd of people, worshiping the Lord with their hands lifted high.

Think about your posture when you worship. Some of us may lift our hands, some of us may close our eyes. No physical stance is more "correct" than another, as long as you are worshiping God as himself. Take inventory of your tendencies, your emotions, your posture during worship.

1 *Ken Coyce, "Habakkuk Chapter 3," Discover Books of the Bible. Last accessed January 27, 2022, https://bible-studys.org/habakkuk-chapter-3/. See also Joshua 3:15.*

Now, think about your posture when you pray. Depending on the day, it may be frantically journaling or merely chatting with God out loud. You may pray before meals or before bed. Take inventory of your tendencies, your emotions, your stance during prayer.

When you pray, do you ask to receive God's gifts, or do you ask to receive more of God himself?

Read Philippians 3:8.

In Philippians, Paul shares that everything apart from knowing Jesus is a loss, a mere waste. The knowledge of Christ Jesus, receiving God himself, is worth more than all things combined.

At the end of Habakkuk 3:13 in the ESV, there's a small cursive word. What is it?

Selah is a call to praise, or a pause to reflect. Let's do this now.

Where have you already seen the Lord move in this transition over the past few weeks?

List works of God the Lord has already shown you (examples of how the Lord has strengthened your faith previously, where he has shown you his power, etc).

Read 1 Corinthians 7:17.

As we walk through this transition, what things do you strive for or work for that the Lord hasn't required of you?

We often live lives based on what we think we should do or what others would approve of. The Lord has a life for you which he crafted with you in mind. Carry that in your prayers this week. Pray, receiving Jesus, trusting his power.

DAY FIVE | Study

Read Habakkuk 3:14-15

In a perfect world, what would you hope to get out of this transition that would allow you to feel "fully" transitioned? (e.g., freedom, peace, a new house, a small group, a feature on your favorite podcast.)

Habakkuk 3:15 brings up the Red Sea again. God, in his great power, parted the sea so his people could pass through it. He didn't abandon his people to die in the wilderness, but made a way to safety. God doesn't leave during our time of need, but remains. He is there, making a way for us.

It is important to note God did not remove the water, but rather split the sea so they could pass through the water. God may not remove something in your life right now, but he will make a way for you to go through it.

Think of the thing or idea you listed above. What would your life look like if you didn't get that?

Do you believe God is still good, powerful, and loving, regardless of what comes next?

Sometimes we understand things cognitively, but do not like it emotionally. The distance between the head and heart can feel like miles. What has kept us from living in and believing the above?

Read Psalm 131.

What do you do to quiet your soul?

When was the last time your soul felt calm?

Where is your hope found?

Read Romans 15:13.

God is a God of hope. Our sure hope is Christ has saved us and we are his forever. Nothing in life is guaranteed, except our citizenship as a son or daughter of God. We are commanded throughout the Scriptures to hope in the Lord and to put our hope in Jesus, and Romans articulates God is the God of hope. He *is* love. And he is good.

Why might it feel hard today to hope in God? What is keeping you from hoping only in God?

DAY SIX | Study

Read Habakkuk 3:16

As I scrolled mindlessly through social media in Bulgaria, it became abundantly clear to me I desired to be viewed as "put together." I wanted to prove myself, to possess competence in the most challenging situation. I did not—and just could not—be the girl peeing herself, but I deeply desired to be the woman seamlessly sauntering the streets of Eastern Europe. Composed, mindful, aware—not an overwhelmed, longing, and crippled girl puttering through the snow-covered sidewalks.

What is something that you feel you must prove, protect, or possess?

When I consider the span of the world, from the beginning to today, from my grandparents' old black-and-white photos to the digital images staring me in the face, a lot has happened. My move, my now few-months in a new country, couldn't be life-crumbling enough to break me, but it felt like it was. These few months reminded me of smallness, yet made me feel like the epicenter of my world.

Habakkuk reveres God. He respects and admires him, and his awareness of the Lord's power compels Habakkuk to also fear God as God. His body trembles and his lips quiver. You know that feeling when your legs feel like jelly, like you're dangling over the edge of a rooftop, a hundred feet in the air? Habakkuk's legs tremble at the presence of God.

Write down the last sentence of verse 16.

The last line in my Bible (ESV) shares Habakkuk "will quietly wait" for the day of trouble. (Habakkuk is waiting for the day of trouble, when people invade them, because that is when God will judge righteously.)

What is something you are waiting for today?

Read Matthew 6:26-34.

Though I know being anxious won't add an hour to my life, it hasn't stopped me from worrying or stressing. God feeds the birds. God loves you more than the birds; God will feed you. God will nourish and care for your mind, body, and spirit. Sometimes we can know things and, like we touched on earlier, it is hard for our hearts to follow.

Consider your answer to the first question from today—the things you may be proving, protecting, possessing, or something you're waiting on.

Knowing God cares for you, how can you surrender these things to Christ?

I often attempt to prove my knowledge or abilities. I know I do not have anything to prove, as my worth rests in God and not in the size of my brain, but I still find myself eager for the chance to provide the right answer or be viewed as competent. I have been working on surrendering this to God by combatting my internal thoughts with Scripture. When a question is asked and I go into performance mode—my palms sweat or my throat begins croaking for significance—I pause. I repeat over and over and over Psalm 46:10, which says, "be still and know that I am God." This is a daily—sometimes hourly—surrender.

Rich Villodas shares, "Those who are poor in spirit have nothing to prove, nothing to protect, nothing to possess. Jesus says the kingdom belongs to these kind of people. People free enough for God to receive the abundance of God's life."[2]

What is keeping you from feeling free today?

2 Richard Villodas, Twitter post, December 10, 2020, 8:48 a.m. Last accessed March 8, 2021, https://twitter.com/richvillodas/status/1337081553370115585.

DAY SEVEN | Reflection

Read Isaiah 58:11-12.

What do you desire to be satisfied?

What—or who—can satisfy that desire?

Read Habakkuk 3:6.

What does this verse reveal about God and his ways?

Read Hebrews 12:1-3.

What do you do for the joy of the Lord?

What do you do from the joy of the Lord?

Thanksgiving + Prayer

What is a prayer for your week? Before you ask of God, honor and glorify who he is in thanksgiving.

Write down a word or phrase for your upcoming week. Not what you feel in this moment, but a word or two to remember who God is.

Have your heart right with Christ, and he will visit you often, and so turn weekdays into Sundays, meals into sacraments, homes into temples, and earth into heaven

- Charles Spurgeon

WEEK FIVE

DAY ONE | Assessment

As I was preparing to begin high school, I quit my lifelong career (moreso a hobby) of cheerleading and decided to try my hand at cross country. I had run track in middle school and was decent at it, and cross country sounded like track but a longer distance.

Choosing cross country felt fairly random, and I didn't even make it through summer conditioning without ending up on crutches. On a misty, humid July morning, we were doing our usual calisthenics in the grass. As we began our karaoke running drill (not the fun, Friday night kind), we turned at the halfway point. Weaving my legs in and out, my whole body twisted while my right foot remained planted.

I fell to the ground in pain. My kneecap sat on the outside of my leg. Season one of cross country was complete.

As much as I thought I was going to quit and never come back—to a sport I was not remotely successful at—I continued on, year after year, showing back up to run. Some seasons were pretty slow and low-key, but cross country was providing more than a way to sweat daily.

My parents' home was walking distance from our high school. Leave the house, turn right. Walk down the long cul-de-sac and hop the fence on the corner. Two crosswalks later, you're there. My older brother had gotten his license that summer and would drive himself to his football practices which began before and ended after cross country. (You can only run for so long; apparently you can do drills all day?)

On the days I wanted to go to practice, an older runner, Megan, offered to pick me up. My home was fairly central in the city, and she drove right by my neighborhood on her way to the high school.

Seasons went on, and eventually we fell into a rhythm of Megan picking me up and dropping me off every day, before and after summer conditioning. If it wasn't obvious from my initial injury, I was never outstanding at cross country. I sat more in the camp of being outstandingly average. Some days I blamed it on an ever-healing injury, but truly I was just more of a middle-of-the-pack runner.

The summer before my senior year, the year after Megan graduated, she invited me to a summer camp with her at a place called Rockbridge. Because I had enjoyed the benefits of Megan's generosity throughout high school (and owed her endless gas money), I said yes.

Prior to this, Megan had invited me to events and activities with other people, who, in her terms, loved Jesus. While I appreciated the inclusivity, loving Jesus was good for her, but I didn't see it as something that was for me.

I had a lot of questions. I had a lot of doubts. I had very little interest in learning about God, and I planned on "getting through" those elements during the week.

One long bus ride and six days of jumping into a lake and hearing about Jesus later—a Jesus who was approachable and merciful; a Jesus I fully needed—I accepted Jesus Christ as the Savior and Lord of my life.

As I grow older, people often ask me my "story" or how I became acquainted with Christ's love.

It always begins like this: "Well, I randomly decided to run cross country."

Write down your journey of how you became acquainted with Christ's love. If you don't consider yourself a follower of Jesus, write down what has led you to this devotional.

What do you understand now, know now, or love more about God, than you did five years ago?

Read Habakkuk 3:17-19.

What stands out to you in these verses?

DAY TWO | Study

Pulse Check: ***How do you feel this week with your current situation?*** *Is this the same answer as week one, or different?*

Read Habakkuk 3:17-19.

Yesterday, I shared a 100-foot view of my story about coming to know my sweet Father. I hope you enjoyed reminiscing on how God brought you to him, as well.

For much of my life, I feel like I've fallen into the group of people who found Jesus in a moment. Snap your fingers. Death to life. Salvation has come. Dunk 'er now.

While it's true that I know the specific date I finally understood the gospel and encountered Jesus, I believe the Lord was working in my heart long before that. Maybe it was easy to understand God's love for me in one evening since my friend Megan had sacrificially served me for three years prior. I also now believe choosing cross country as my post-cheerleading sport was not mere coincidence. God graciously had his hand on my life, long before I was aware of it. What felt like a spur-of-the-moment sport switcharoo turned into an eternal impact on earth.

Sometimes, we understand life better in retrospect. Sometimes, we see God's hand after the fact. What is an example of something you didn't understand or enjoy in the moment, but now has purpose, or makes sense in retrospect?

Read Romans 8:18-19.

What earthly thing do you feel like you are longing for today?

What is the future glory mentioned in 8:18?

How can or how should your mindset shift knowing that our future glory is a perfect heaven with a loving Father?

Read Romans 8:31-32.

God gave his son for us. God gave his son for you. Jesus is better than the most beautiful piece of jewelry or a new car or security in your current situation.

How can we hope differently in light of that?

DAY THREE | Study

Read Habakkuk 3:17

Habakkuk walks us through the necessities of life—the food needed for survival—but there are no elements of life to be found at this time. The trees aren't blossoming, and there's no fruit nor olive produce nor cattle to be found. It's a dire situation.

List some necessities for your life.

Because we've now read Habakkuk 3:17-19 a few times, we know what's coming; but we will save the "yet" for tomorrow.

How do you feel when you're lacking one (or several) of the necessities you listed above?

There was a season of my pre-teens where I really wanted a white-jean purse. I simply had to have it. My parents, unwavered by a fad, would not buy me the purse. I was livid. In my mind, if they loved me, they would want me to be happy. Happiness would be brought to me through the white jean purse (obviously), and I didn't know why they couldn't see that.

The purse was clearly a want, not a necessity. Our necessities, like food and water and a warm home, are important to life here on earth. As humans on earth, it can be easy to connect the fulfillment of our necessities to God's level of love for us. God's love is different from human love, though; it does not change depending on how our earthly life appears.

Read Romans 8:35.

We are unable to remove, detach, or separate ourselves from God's love. Sure, we can ignore it. We can focus on what we lack, dwelling on a few things from our list above. Even still, it is impossible to prevent God from loving us.

What is distracting you from the love of Christ in this season of life?

Let's continue in Romans. **Read Romans 8:38-39.**

Because of this, how can you hope, trust, and pray differently?

Which of your fears would subside with the knowledge that you are loved, recklessly and wholly, by God? Which fears still exist?

DAY FOUR | Study

Read Habakkuk 3:18

What does rejoicing look like or mean to you?

Habakkuk lists things that are hard. Times are sad. Events are devastating. But Habakkuk also reveals his greatest joy: God. After wrestling with God for a while, Habakkuk is no longer discouraged by his circumstances and situation. His faith and joy are found in the Lord: solely in God himself.

Despite your circumstances, why can you take joy in God today?

Joy is a hard concept for me to understand, as I want to associate it with laughing and smiling and enjoying every moment. That's what joy is, right? However, Habakkuk shows us a different kind of joy. A joy that is found inwardly, peacefully, resting fully in God and salvation.

Do you feel rested and/or joyful today? Why or why not?

At some point in college, I lost a lot of sleep and rest due to fear and anxiousness, both rooted in a deep mistrust and distorted view of Jesus. As opposed to finding joy in God himself, I found joy in the gifts God gave me. When my circumstances changed drastically as I walked through a break-up, the death of a friend, and a brutal semester, my view of God changed drastically.

Read Psalm 56:3-4.

What are those infinite, ***never-changing characteristics*** *of the Lord we can cling to amid uncertainty?*

DAY FIVE | Study

Read Habakkuk 3:19

What does Habakkuk say God is to him in the first line?

Habakkuk says God makes his feet like a deer's feet. Deer can walk and scale heights without slipping, which parallels Habakkuk's faith in the Lord: firm. After walking through his questions with God, Habakkuk knows God is his strength and has made his faith firm.

In what ways have you seen your faith change over the past few weeks?

In what parts of this transition have you seen the Lord already work?

Even if you haven't seen hints of it yet, the season you're walking through will come to know the glory of God. Every inch of the earth was created to proclaim Jesus. He will bring glory through this transition, and he will be glorified through your faithfulness to him.

What is preventing you from being able to claim God as your sole strength and glory?

Read Psalm 19:1-6.

What does it look like for you to glorify God in your daily life?

How could you do this without words, like in the Psalm above? ("They have no speech; they use no words; no sound is heard from them.") What does this suggest?

Write a praise to God. This could be anything, like praising God for his glory or his faithfulness to his people.

DAY SIX | Study

Read Habakkuk 3:17-19

If you wrote verse 17, what might it say? Despite it, in what pain do you rejoice in Jesus?

Read Matthew 6:25.

Matthew 6:25 closes with, "Is not life more than food, and the body more than clothing?" Jesus tells us our lives and our bodies have a greater purpose than just enjoying good food and showing off the latest fashion trends.

What do you think your life is for? Similarly, what is your body for?

Paul wrote 1 and 2 Corinthians to the church at Corinth. 1 Corinthians focuses on practical questions, like spiritual gifts or marriage, and 2 Corinthians expands on those issues. If you've been to a wedding recently, you've probably heard Scripture cited from 1 Corinthians (love is patient, love is kind, anyone?).

Read 1 Corinthians 6:19-20.

In 2 Corinthians 1:5-6, in a section titled "God of All Comfort," Paul writes:

For as we share abundantly in Christ's sufferings, so through Christ we share abundantly in comfort too. If we are afflicted, it is for your comfort and salvation; and if we are comforted, it is for your comfort, which you experience when you patiently endure the same sufferings that we suffer.

To be expectant of the Lord means to be patient and wait faithfully for the Lord to move. In what areas of your life are you expectant of the Lord?

In what areas of your life are you relying on the Lord?

In what areas of your life are you asking the Lord for a greater fulfillment?

Read Lamentations 3:22-23.

Practically, what does the Lord's faithfulness mean to you in this season?

Pray over and contemplate this today. Consider asking the Spirit to fill you. Even if you got the things listed above, even if the fig tree blossomed, God is nourishment. In plenty or want, God is satisfying. Eternal hope is found in God.

DAY SEVEN | Reflection

I wouldn't go back to the day my kneecap dislocated if I were paid $1,000. I still wince when I remember the sliding and clicking of my joints as I fell to the damp grass. Despite my mediocre seasons, some good came from cross country. I would go back for the realization of my Father every day. I believe the Lord will bring us to him, and he will teach us what we need to know, despite where we live or what obstacles might be in the way.

Would I eventually have come to know the love of Jesus if I hadn't run cross country? Sure. But I am so thankful the Father drew me to himself the way he did.

Would the Lord have eventually led me to a counselor's office to heal after Bulgaria if I had gone to a different country or had come home to a different city? Probably. But I am so thankful the Father helped me use godly resources when he did.

Jesus is teaching you something. While you may have been able to learn this in a different way, he is walking through this with you. There's great celebration in this truth, and if you can't find a reason for celebration in your situation today, there's always a reason in God himself.

Read Habakkuk 3:17-19.

Who has the Lord been for you during this transition? List the specific characteristics of God you have experienced during this season.

If you have not been able to see the Lord's hand in your transition, in what ways do you still believe his very nature is good?

If not, what is preventing you from believing that?

Read Hebrews 10:23-25.

What keeps you from holding onto hope in this transition?

In order to praise God in a transition, what do you need to accept of him? (e.g., that he is faithful, with me, has gone before me, etc.)

What practices can you introduce into your life to praise God daily?

Thanksgiving + Prayer

What is a prayer for your week? Before you ask of God, honor and glorify who he is in thanksgiving.

Write down a word or phrase for your upcoming week. Not what you feel in this moment, but a word or two to remember who God is.

Never be afraid to trust an unknown future to a known God.

– Corrie Ten Boom

WEEK SIX

DAY ONE | Assessment

Every July 3rd, I wake up and drive to Chick-fil-A. I park my car, walk inside, and order exactly what I ordered that July 3rd I returned from Bulgaria—sometimes with extra hashbrowns. If I have time, I'll sit inside and eat breakfast; but if work or meetings beckon, I'll grab it to go and get back into my car.

As I remember the exhaustion, the tears, and the adjustment, I pause. The salt of the chicken and the warm butter on the roll soothes me. It reminds me what the Lord has done in the last year, two years, and even the last several years.

Every year I go to Chick-fil-A as some sort of commemoration of the past. A commemoration of making it through a season so wavy and tumultuous, I didn't know what the other side looked like. Every year I go as a way to honor the past while still living in the present. It gives me a methodical and kind way to remember Bulgaria—the things it gave me, the things it changed in me, and the things it took from me. It gives me a way to remember a beautiful season of life without straddling the in-between forever.

We can appreciate and honor the hardships, the pain, and the past, yet firmly believe God is good, kind, and wholly present.

Read Habakkuk 1:2.

Habakkuk starts with a complaint to God and ends with rejoicing in God. His pain hasn't fully left, yet he takes joy in God.

Read Habakkuk 3:17-18.

The last several weeks have been a journey, paralleled with your season of transition. Turn back to page 68. What was the complaint and prayer you wrote?

In what ways have you specifically seen the Lord act over that in the past several weeks?

Read Matthew 7:7-8.

In your life and in this season of transition, what still feels unsettled or in process?

DAY TWO | God Listens

Read Habakkuk 1:10-11, 2:18-19

These verses show a Father who listens. He lists and acknowledges specific things Habakkuk says and worries about. God listens by asking questions like, "What profit is an idol when its maker has shaped it, a metal image, a teacher of lies?" God asking questions in return shows that he is actively listening to Habakkuk's complaints and following up on specific elements. This active listening shows the intentionality of God.

Sophia, my younger sister who has been interviewing for physical therapy schools, recently explained she really likes when interviewers ask follow-up questions to her responses. She elaborated by saying she is thankful when they go "off-script" in this way, because it shows her they really listened to her.

In what ways do you enjoy feeling heard? In what specific ways does your family or friends make you feel listened to (or not listened to)?

Read Jeremiah 29:11-13.

The difference between our family and friends listening to us and the God of the universe listening to us is that God knows the plans he has for us (Jer 29:11). When our family and friends listen, they can only hope for our future. They typically only hope for things they can see or have experienced, like finding a good partner or getting a job offer. The Lord knows our future. The Lord knows our desires, wants, needs, and the deepest places of our hearts. God is sovereign and holy, desiring for us a future and a hope. God cares about our present life, and he also cares about our next life in heaven. God listens, already knowing what's to come.

How do the verses in Jeremiah characterize God?

Read 1 John 5:13-15.

How has your confidence in God changed during your transition?

Knowing that God actively listens to you, how does this change the way you pray?

DAY THREE | God Cares

Read Habakkuk 2:2, 2:4, 2:20

Outside of your specific prayers, where else have you seen Jesus throughout this transition?

What characteristics of Jesus have been revealed to you?

I hope you have seen that God cares. God cares about your seasons of transition and your current walk with him; but more so, he cares for *you*. The God of the Universe not only listens, but deeply cares about you.

God shows his care for us daily in life and throughout the Bible. Jesus was brutally killed (crucified) out of love for us. After his resurrection, Jesus gave us the Great Commission. In this, Jesus shows God's great care for us, as he is giving us instructions on how he wants us to live as God's children in the world.

Read Matthew 28:16-20.

The powerful, almighty God of the Universe intricately cares about you and your day-to-day life. Because God cares about his children (us), he shows us in the Scriptures how we are to live. Paul furthers this idea and gives us additional things to ponder in Philippians.

Read Philippians 4:8-9.

For something to be commendable means it is deserving of praise. What is something commendable to you?

How can your actions and thoughts match what's commendable?

DAY FOUR | We Wait

Read Habakkuk 2:1, 3:16

Both of these verses discuss Habakkuk waiting. All throughout Scripture, there are stories of the Lord's people waiting on God for deliverance from struggles, for healing, and for the return of the Messiah.

Read Malachi 4:5-6.

These are the last few words of the Old Testament. After the Old Testament comes the New Testament, beginning with Matthew. Between that page-turn, though, lies nearly 400 years of silence from the audible voice of God.

The people of God who lived and died during this 400-year period of silence waited their whole lifetime for him. In what ways can you wait for the Lord to move in this transition season?

I am not prone to patience. I love understanding, efficiency, and speed. As I work through patience, time in prayer has reminded me why I'm comfortable waiting: the Lord's power, love, and peace he gives. The more I've learned to trust my Maker, the more I naturally fall into the verses we've read—naturally listening to God—like Jeremiah 29:12.

Read Isaiah 8:17.

Throughout this devotional, there have been words highlighted in ***dark blue.*** Use these words to fill in the blanks below, creating a prayer that reflects this season of transition. In cases where the *questions* are ***dark blue***, the answers—*your words*—are what will be used in the blank spaces. By pairing your experiences throughout the last several weeks with the Lord's unchanging words, this exercise will create a unique prayer. When words are sparse, I pray this will serve as a tool for you to talk to the Father.

Father, you are __________ *and my* ______________________________ .
(pg 30) week 1 day 2 — (pg 36) week 1 day 4 Ps. 46:1

You are __________, *even when my situation doesn't feel that way.*
(pg 36) week 1 day 4 Ps. 34:8

God, I ask to see your heart for me today. You are a __________ ,
(pg 44) week 1 day 6

______________ , *and* ____________ *God.*
(pg 44) week 1 day 6 — (pg 44) week 1 day 6

Even though I have felt ____________________ (pg 26) week 1 day 1,

____________________ (pg 92) week 3 day 2, and ____________________ (pg 158) week 5 day 2,

you are ____________________ (pg 166) week 5 day 4.

Lord, I remember and praise you for ____________________

____________________ (pg 131) week 4 day 3.

I thank you for ____________________

____________________ (pg 79) week 2 day 7.

Lord, though I long for ____________________ (pg 105) week 3 day 5,

I know you have asked me to ____________ (pg 70) week 2 day 5. You, God, are the

ultimate gift. God, help me to ____________________ (pg 99) week 3 day 4.

Lord, help me do what you've asked. I will ____________________ (pg 40) week 1 day 5

your faithful hand at work.

In Jesus' name,

Amen

....

DAY FIVE | God Loves

Read Habakkuk 3:13-15

Write down the first sentence of verse 13 below.

My ESV Bible reads, "You went out for the salvation of your people, for the salvation of your anointed."

In your own words, explain what it means that God "went out" for your salvation.

These verses depict God's great love for us. God went out to save his people from themselves. That is godly, sovereign love. Verses 13-15 also show the Lord's great power—power that has trampled the sea. In his great power, we see his great love for us. His great love for us is this: while we were helpless and hopeless with destructive and disgruntled souls, Jesus came to earth—fully God and fully man—and lived a sinless life. He walked the earth you are walking now and never sinned. That means Jesus never lied nor cussed nor cheated. He was perfect in every way and still understands what humans experience on earth.

Since we are sinful people, we cannot go to heaven on our own. No amount of trying or striving can get us to a perfect place because we are tainted, imperfect people. If you put one drop of food coloring, just one, into a gallon jug of water, the water is no longer perfectly clear. Regardless of the shade of the water, a light hue or deep tone, the water is not clear; it is no longer pure nor perfect.

Regardless of your sin, a speeding ticket or a series of broken relationships, you cannot get to heaven on your own. Given our sin, we need a substitute. God loves us so much he sent Jesus, our perfect and blameless substitute, to be crucified on the cross for you.

Now, if you are a believer and follower of Jesus Christ, when you reach the gate of heaven, Jesus is with you. Jesus covers you, allowing God to invite you into eternal joy in heaven.

"Well done, good and faithful servant" will be giddily expressed and celebrated as you walk through.

Read John 3:16-18.

If you believe in the work of Jesus on the cross, you will not be condemned. Through Jesus dying on the cross, you are freed from sin. Describe what this means to you.

God is powerful. God is more powerful than the storms of transition. And God is sacrificial, giving his only Son, so people on earth would be redeemed and brought near God.

Read John 19:30.

Jesus, a blameless and sinless man, gave up his life so we could have life to the full, a fullness of joy for the body and soul. God lovingly and purposefully fulfilled his promise to redeem the souls of man—and he is still fulfilling that promise today.[1]

1 *See Genesis 3:15, Psalm 110, Romans 16:20, Revelation 20:1-2, 1 Corinthians 15:28.*

Jesus's life on earth began in a manger and ended in resurrection.

There is a beginning and an end to our time on earth. Both will come, and both will pass. There is a beginning and an end to this season of transition. Both will come, and both will pass. The Lord holds both end caps and everything in between.

God, acting as book-ends on our life, sees the entire story. Just as we have read through the entirety of Habakkuk, we understand it and can see Habakkuk's broader story. The book of Habakkuk as a whole makes sense, but if we just picked out a random verse, we would be without the context and might be left confused.

Picture God holding your life, like the way you might be holding this book in your hands. God is able to see and protect the entirety of what you are walking through.

In what ways would your life change (maybe even practically) from trusting this?

DAY SIX | God Answers

Read Habakkuk 1:5, 2:2-3

Read Philippians 4:19-20.

What verbs are listed in these verses? In other words, what words detail God's actions in these verses?

God answers his people. He asks for us to look and to be astounded and wait for his vision, but he does answer us.

Throughout your walk with God, what is something he has "answered" in your life?

Throughout the Bible, God answers his people. He delivers them from illness, blesses them with children, and provides clarity to questions. He uses everything, even things like injustice, to draw his people to himself.

Like I mentioned earlier, one of the clearest moments God answers and fulfills his word is when Jesus comes after 400 years of silence.

Yesterday, we read about what Jesus coming meant to the world. Now, let's go back hundreds of years before Jesus was born.

Read Isaiah 7:10-14.

Isaiah says the Lord himself will give you a sign. In this scenario, a sign is an answer. That sign, Immanuel—Jesus in the flesh—did not come for years. We neither see nor understand what God sees and understands. We rely on hindsight or faith to provide clarity. It's okay to ask what or why or how long; we see that throughout Scripture. But we trust God through the uncertainty, as God has shown his trustworthiness through giving the world Jesus, his only son.

Read Acts 13:41.

What verse does this remind you of?

How does this verse characterize God?

What does this truth mean for you?

DAY SEVEN | We Rejoice + Proclaim

Read Habakkuk 3:19

Throughout the book of Habakkuk, we've seen doubt and confusion transform into desire for and clarity in God. We see a man rejoice in and proclaim who God is.

Rewrite Habakkuk 3:19 in your own words.

What tangible actions can you do, or thoughts can you hold onto, to remember the transformation of Habakkuk in your transition? How will this impact your prayer and thought life?

Read Colossians 1:24-26.

In the above Scripture, Paul (who also wrote Philippians) writes to the church in Colossae to show the grandeur of God. Paul shares he rejoices in his sufferings for the potential to make God known to people. He doesn't just tolerate the pain, but rejoices in it for the sake of the gospel.

Write down a few events occurring in the upcoming days and months. These can be events that make you anxious, excited, or sad.

What do you need to remember about God's character over the coming weeks?

Read Philippians 4:4-7.

In the midst of this transition in your life, you've spent the last month and a half with God. You've read through an Old Testament book, Habakkuk (multiple times, might I add), and you've read countless verses throughout Scripture.

Take a moment to thank God for his word and helping prioritize your faith in an unsteady season.

Take a moment to thank God for his grace and generosity in caring for you.

As we depart from the structured daily routine with God, decide on the next book of Scripture that will continue carrying you. Being with the Lord daily—the consistency of honoring him and building up your foundation of faith—is critically important.

We, quite literally, walk by faith, not by sight (2 Corinthians 5:7).

Read John 8:12.

In what can you rejoice today?

For though I am free from all, I have made myself a servant to all, that I might win more of them. To the Jews I became as a Jew, in order to win Jews. To those under the law I became as one under the law (though not being myself under the law) that I might win those under the law. To those outside the law I became as one outside the law (not being outside the law of God but under the law of Christ) that I might win those outside the law. To the weak I became weak, that I might win the weak. I have become all things to all people, that by all means I might save some. I do it all for the sake of the gospel, that I may share with them in its blessings.

- 1 Corinthians 9:19-23

A Note from the Author | Epilogue

Hey Friend,

If you have finished all six weeks of the study, I pray you feel a sense of peace.

I do not know if you are exhausted and burnt-out, or inspired and encouraged; but my deepest wish for you is peace in who you are—and what you have—in Christ.

In my most volatile, painfully-adjusting seasons, I wanted someone to tell me it would be okay; but when they did, I didn't believe them. My hope for you is through God's Word and with God himself, you know it will be okay and it is well. Things lost on this side of heaven may not return, but we can deeply rejoice over what's found in our Father.

I want to acknowledge a few things as we wrap up.

First, the obvious: timing. Your transition might not have fit seamlessly within this six-week time period. If you are still in the middle of this period, please know that over the last month and a half, you've poured into yourself the best way possible: by letting Jesus pour into you. More than the things the world tells us, like doing our squats or color-coding a shelf could ever heal us and bring peace, you've shown up and answered some challenging, reflective questions over the last several weeks. For that, and for your willingness to walk the windy road, I'm proud of and grateful for you.

If your transition is still ongoing, or if you're curious where to head next in the Bible, I have listed several of my favorite books below, some of which we have already read snippets of throughout this study. Truly, though, there isn't a bad book found within the Bible. Continue your momentum in the Word, learning more about who God is, and I pray you discover the freedom that is yours to be had on earth. Some recommendations below:

- *Psalms*
- *Romans*
- *Philippians*
- *Hebrews*
- *Isaiah*
- *1 Corinthians*
- *Matthew*

Secondly, while this was mentioned throughout, I want to be clear: transitions can bring painful parts of life to the surface. This can also involve or magnify anxiety, depression, your ability to sleep, and your mental health as a whole. If you are struggling or feel deeply alone, I would highly encourage you to seek out a counselor in your area.

When I returned home from my year in Bulgaria, my life was exceptionally gray with sprouts of pain popping up everywhere I looked. Seeing and working with my Christian counselor was invaluable. She helped me walk through my anxiousness and get back on my feet when it truly felt impossible just months earlier. This book would not have been possible without the hours I spent in her office, and for that I'm endlessly grateful.

While Jesus and I were writing this devotional, I've also been a part-time student, specifically studying leadership. In a class recently, we were discussing career adjustment and the ways adults transition to (or from) leadership. Paraphrased, a classmate shared: "To be in transit is to be in the process of leaving one thing without having fully left it, and, at the same time, entering something else without fully being a part of it."

My stomach panged, as I know the feelings of straddling spaces, emotions, and seasons of life. Transition—and this journey of life—morphs and continues until we reach our Father in heaven, where we will be fully and wholly a part of what our soul has longed for. Take heart: you are a part of the Lord's family. You are fully a part of the kingdom of God, a beloved child.

Lastly, please know God, the Creator of the Universe, our Strength, our Conqueror over death, can handle your questions. He can handle your complaints, your frustration, and your exhaustion. We serve a God who wants to answer us, who gives rest to the weary, and hope to the brokenhearted.

This God, the God who turned my bitterness to joy and my confusion to clarity, is the God who wants to walk through every transition season with you.

My prayer for you is you will come to know God intimately; that you will fall more in love with him. My prayer is you will rejoice in the Lord. He's not done working on you yet. I'm praying for you.

In him,

E

About The Author

Erica spends her days as a consultant and her evenings as a doctoral student, yet her favorite roles are being a daughter, sister, and friend. You can find her yelling "Roll Tide!" at a television, enjoying a long run, or writing—probably wrapped in a fuzzy blanket. An alumna of the Fulbright Program, she loves traveling and seeing the consistency of God and his love for people throughout the world. Yet: The Promise in Habakkuk for Those in Transition, is her first published devotional.